THE
BY THE LAKE

Written by Antonella Parisi

Celebration Press
An Imprint of Pearson Learning

Chicago has a very special aquarium. Thousands of people visit it each day to see the amazing ocean animals from all over the world.

The Shedd Aquarium is one of the few places in the Midwest where you can see marine mammals. Dolphins, whales, seals, and sea otters are all part of a unique exhibit called the *Oceanarium*.

People call the aquarium the "Ocean by the Lake" because there is an ocean exhibit inside and a lake outside.

Tide pools and deep water exhibits make it possible to see a variety of ocean life. This includes tiny shrimp and crabs, and larger animals such as seals and penguins.

Other fascinating species that live at the Shedd are beluga whales and Pacific white-sided dolphins. There are many things to learn about all these ocean mammals, from the way they communicate to the way they move through the water.

Belugas are smaller than other types of whales. Full-grown belugas weigh about 3,000 pounds and are 12 to 16 feet long. Although they are gray at birth, they later become completely white.

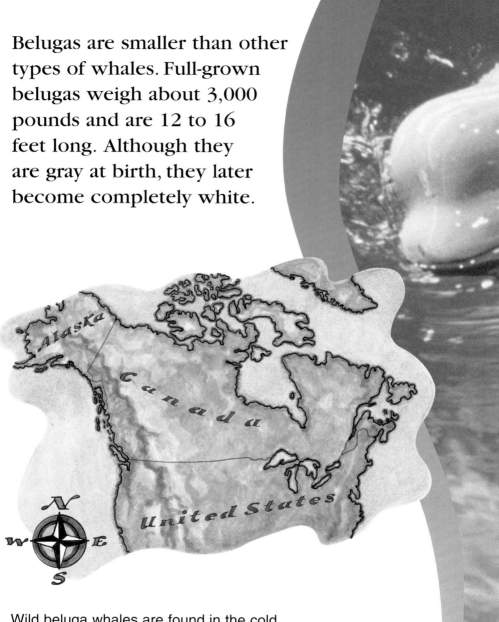

Wild beluga whales are found in the cold waters of Alaska and Hudson Bay, off the coast of Canada, and in the St. Lawrence River.

Belugas have a bony ridge on their backs that helps them cut through icy water. They also use it to punch holes in the ice when they need to come to the surface to breathe.

Belugas have a large forehead, called a *melon*, and a *blowhole* for breathing and communicating. Scientists have recorded hundreds of different sounds belugas can make using their blowholes.

Pacific white-sided dolphins are small. They are 6 to 7 feet long and weigh about 220 to 300 pounds when fully grown. Like whales, dolphins make many sounds with their blowholes. They feed on many different types of fish and small ocean animals, such as krill.

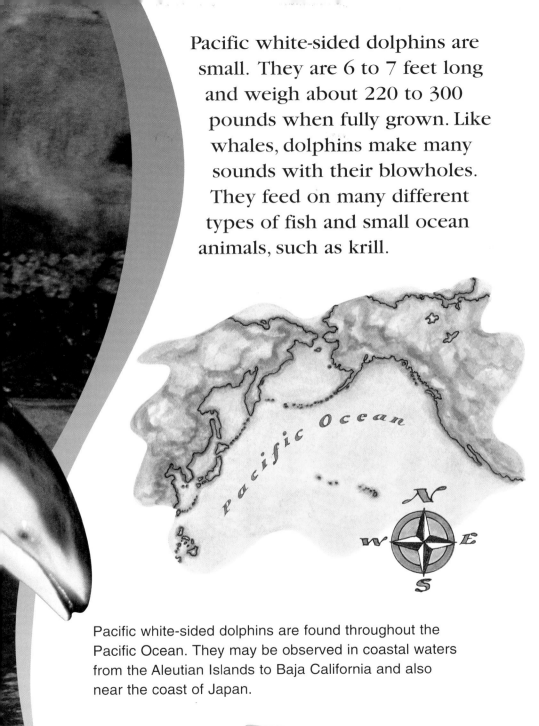

Pacific white-sided dolphins are found throughout the Pacific Ocean. They may be observed in coastal waters from the Aleutian Islands to Baja California and also near the coast of Japan.

Pacific white-sided dolphins have bold markings. Their black backs and white bellies help them to hide from predators. This kind of coloring is called *countershading*.

Dolphins have a lot of energy and often somersault through the air. With an arrow-shaped body and strong tail, they can reach speeds up to 25 m.p.h.

In the wild, whales and dolphins must learn to hunt for food and watch out for predators.

At the Shedd Aquarium, the whales and dolphins have the help of the animal care specialists who feed and check them each day.

In a typical day, the animal care specialists at the aquarium will work with the animals on several routine exercises.

For instance, marine mammals have "play visits" to the veterinarian every day. The trainer makes a game of checking each animal's teeth, tongue, body, and tail.

By playing this game, the whales and dolphins get used to seeing the doctor and are not afraid. Unlike wild whales and dolphins, these marine mammals live longer and healthier lives because of the veterinary care they receive.

Whales and dolphins often leap out of the water and land on their sides. This is called *breaching*, and may be a way of warning others in the group. It might even be a way of scratching an itch on the skin!

Sometimes whales and dolphins slap their tail on the water. This is called *tail lobbing*. Vibrations from these sounds travel through water for miles and may be another way marine mammals talk with one another.

Ocean mammals can also jump completely out of the water and reach amazing heights. This is known as *porpoising*. These jumps enable the animals to observe what's happening above the surface.

The Shedd's trainers are very important in the whales' and dolphins' daily routine. These animal care specialists feed and take care of the animals. A close relationship grows between the animals and their trainers.

The animal care specialists have spent years studying marine mammals and their environments. They share their interest in these mammals with the people who visit the aquarium.

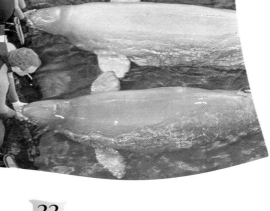

A trip to the Shedd
Aquarium is like a trip
to the ocean. When
we learn about ocean
mammals, we learn
more about our world.